THE PROBLEM OF LEFTHANDEDNESS

For Medical-Therapeutic Eurythmy Work

Excerpts and Contributions
Compiled and with an Introduction
by Gerda Hueck

Translated by R.E.M. Finser

RSCP

Originally published by the Heileurythmie-Ausbildung, Stuttgart, Germany, 1978.

FIRST EDITION
St. George Publications, Spring Valley, New York, by permission of the Schriftenreihe der Heileurythmie-Ausbildung, Stuttgart, Germany, 1978

Cover design by Florin Lowndes redrawn from the original

ISBN 0-916786-83-8

Reprinted 2002

Copyright © 1986 by Ruth E.M. Finser

All rights in this book are reserved. No part of this publication may be reproduced in any form, stored in a retrieval system, or transmitted, in any form, or by any means, electronic-mechanical, photocopying, recording or otherwise without the prior written permission of the publisher except for brief quotations embodied in critical articles for reviews.

Book orders:
Rudolf Steiner College Bookstore:
Tel 916-961-8729 FAX 916-961-3032
E-mail: bookstore@steinercollege.edu

Rudolf Steiner College Press, 9200 Fair Oaks Boulevard, Fair Oaks, CA 95628

INTRODUCTION

The problem of lefthandedness confronts parents, kindergarten teachers, class teachers, therapeutic eurythmists and doctors. If the changeover to righthandedness, especially for writing, is to be attempted, then one needs to find an individual solution for each child.
Rudolf Steiner gave fundamental indications for 'changing over' at conferences for Waldorf school teachers and at lectures, in which he gave important insights for recognizing qualitative differences between the right and left in the human form and in space. Through the many-sided variety of explanations, the educator is able to learn of the many different levels which are inherent in this problem. Many of these excerpts from the conferences and lectures were printed in the periodical *Menschenschule* (School for Humanity) (the Swiss Waldorf School teachers educational journal) 1930, 1954 and 1970. The *Rudolf Steiner*

Nachlassverwaltung has agreed that these excerpts could be taken out of the lectures and published here. They constitute the main part of this publication and, for an in-depth study, we recommend the reading of the entire lecture.

Dr. Rudolf Braumiller gave a lecture on April 20, 1977 during the doctors' conference (in Bad Teinach, Germany) on the question of 'dominance' in the practice of school doctors. In this publication, he introduces the problem from a similar point of view.

The therapeutic eurythmist, Ilse Rolofs, speaks about the problem from her many years of experience at schools. She passed on her experiences to therapeutic eurythmists in many training courses.

From her experience at the Kraeherwald Waldorf School in Stuttgart, Brigitte Schuerholz is able to give a very specific contribution. Through this contribution, we can experience very specifically how it is possible to perceive the child with his own awakened particular will and how the exercises were created. It is hoped that this publication will be a stimulus for many therapeutic eurythmists and encourage them to characterize and exchange experiences in their own work with left-handed children, and thus help to develop a deeper insight into the destiny of these children.

Gerda Hueck

The Question of Sidedness

The questions that arise while changing a 'left-hander' are not yet satisfactorily clarified. However, research has produced a great many new facts during the past decades.

All conscious sense activity and the movements of one side of the body are projected through images to the opposite side of the brain as a result of the crossing of nerve tracts. In the right-handed person, the left half of the brain assumes a 'dominant' position. Almost one-third of the surface of the motor projection of the cerebral cortex is taken up by the hand and fingers. Finger movement is foremost in evolution. M. Kolzova and L.W. Fomina (Leningrad)[1] noted that the development of speech was in direct relationship to the movement of the fingers. "Children who succeed in making isolated movements with their fingers are 'speaking children'."

---
[1] in *Der Kinderarzt*, June, 1975

Especially significant is the moment when the opposition of the thumb begins. From then on, the child can make delicately differentiated movements. The foundation of the succeeding speech formation is laid when the finger movements develop. Once speech is acquired, the brain can become the organ (the tool) of intelligence. I.M. Ssetschenov and I. Pavlov were of the opinion that the muscular perceptions of the speech organism were of importance for thinking. The movements and gestures of the right hand are experienced by the left half of the brain. The hand forms the foundation for the dominance of one brain hemisphere over the other.

When there were seriously ill people (they suffered from epilepsy)[2], one had to sever the cross-connection *(corpus callosum)* of the two hemispheres. One could then study the isolated workings of each half of the brain, and found great qualitative differences (with right-handed people). In these experiments, one allowed right and left hands to touch things separately: also, the right and left sides of the face were separated by a wall. For instance, the

---
[2]from *Bild der Wissenschaft*, September, 1972

patient was given the word, "heart." It was written in such a way that "art" was to the right of the point of fixation and "he" was on the left. The patient said, "art" (for this he used the left side of the brain). On cards, he searched with the left hand for the "he." J. Bogen further found that the patient could write with the right hand but he could no longer draw well with it. If he had to draw a square, he drew all four corners with connections on top of each other. The left hand, however, could draw and copy spatial forms, but could not copy a written word! The left hand can work with wholeness but does not have the capacity to assimilate verbal analytical information. The non-verbal reactions of the left side proceed more quickly. With the construction of a two-dimensional figure with dice, it is successful when the left hand helps the right. If one has to describe pictorial material from the left side of facial vision in words, one gathers the impression that it is not perceived. The experiment has a different result if one asks the patient not to describe the object seen with words, but to select it from among many illustrations or to 'feel' it with the left hand from among a number of objects. Then the left hand locates the correct object. But the patient nevertheless insists that he does not know what he is holding in his left hand.

To summarize:

Brain, right (= left half of body)	Brain, left (= right half of body)
Space, bodily perception 'whole'	Time, speech, 'knowledge'
Simultaneous, more diffuse assimilation of a lot of information, fast (outer world*)	Analytical and logical
	Linear, successive assimilation of information, slower (ego-experience on the outer world*)

  In the act of seeing, the images perceived through each eye cross each other as a result of the crossing of many of the fibers of the optic nerve and, therefore, are projected as one image on the visual cortex part of the brain. It is due to the fact that two images become one that depth perception becomes a possibility for a person. (A one-eyed person, for instance, can have difficulty in judging the distance of an approaching car!) For the human being, an ego-experience is taking place in space.

---
*by the author

When one is very tired, one has a dimming of consciousness; also in intoxication, the perception is disturbed: one can see double! Such a 'touching of oneself' as it happens in vision in a 'fixed' manner takes place in all sense perception and in feelings of the right and left halves of the body. When we fold our hands, the sense of touch helps us to concentrate and focus inwardly. We have a comprehensive description of these processes in Rudolf Steiner's lecture of April 9, 1920.

Since most people have become righthanded, sense perception turns more toward the left side of the body, therefore, more toward the external world. The right side follows; it serves simultaneously to perceive the 'self' and thereby produce ego representation. When a child develops righthandedness at the beginning of the school years, or even earlier when imitating drawing and painting, the speech centers, which are originally potentially present in both cerebral hemispheres, will now only be utilized on the left side of the brain. Therefore, the left hemisphere gains complete control over speech (Broca's Area), and comprehension of speech

(Wernicke's Area), gains dominance over the right side of the brain.

V. Arnim, in "The Child in Need of Special Care" (vol. 15 #2 of the quarterly journal *Seelenpflege Bedurftige Kind*) writes: "It seems that a mirror picture symmetrical function of limbs and sense organs is sufficient in order to organize one's actions and one's body in three-dimensional space, as it is in the animal (monkeys are ambidextrous). However, the visualization of space and mental activities seems to need an asymmetry, that is a lateralization (i.e., an establishment of dominance for the opposite side of the brain)." This step in the development of the child seems to begin when the child is ready for school. An examination of three- to five-year olds revealed the fact that, when they were looking at pictures (not while they were drawing), they tilted their heads from 90 to 180 degrees. This stopped between the ages of six to seven.[3]

H. Woelfflin[4] shows that while adults were viewing Rembrandt's picture *Three Trees*, they were looking at it from left to right. This picture would lose its effect if

---
[3]in M. Sovak *Pedagogische Probleme der Lateralitat (Volk und Gesundheit, Berlin)*

[4]from *Sandorama*, April, 1972

one were to look at it in a mirror. It is different with East Asian art which pictures movement from right to left and it, therefore, leaves a 'flat impression'. Perspective matters very little here. At the beginning of the last century, it was already noted in Africa, Central and South America that European posters were, for the most part, falsely seen and misunderstood by the people. Meanwhile, it has been ascertained that black school children perceived spatial depth in pictures more accurately than did illiterate adults! There is extensive evidence that unlettered Africans are unable to 'interpret' flat representations in a spatial way. It becomes clear that there is a connection between learning to write with the right hand, the ability to see perspective and the development of the intellect. With 'lateralization'; one can grasp spatial depth consciously. This may be one of the many causes of dyslexia. L. Schenk-Danzinger says that "it is commonly accepted today that the extent of lateralization has something to do with the capacity of the child to learn the symbols of letters and numbers and to learn to read and write fluently."[5]

---

[5]in *Handbuch der Legastenie im Kindesalter*, Weinheim, 1968

Our present-day 'abductive' writing (directed away from the body) is in accord with righthandedness. Mirror writing is a left-handed 'abductive' writing. O. Poetzl illustrated the connection between hemispheric dominance and the direction of writing in the course of human development.[6] The oldest historical writings were written from top to bottom (Chinese, Egyptian, Korean, Japanese) or from right to left (Etruscan, East Indian, Semitic). There are even transitional periods in Greek and Latin inscriptions with a kind of 'meander' writing (going back and forth)! Greek writing became 'flowing to the right' in the fifth century B.C. We can see hereby that the emphasis on writing with the right hand coincided with the beginning of the Intellectual Soul Age, which stands under the sign of Aries and was influenced by Mars (747 B.C. to 1413 A.D.). This is in contrast to the eastern, Asiatic soul attitude which was still represented in the sixth century B.C. by Lao-Tse: "When the wise man is at home, he treasures the left; if he needs weapons, he treasures the right. Weapons are tools of disaster, not tools of

---

[6]op. cit.³

wise men ... Happy actions prefer the left, painful actions prefer the right."[3]

I will summarize Rudolf Steiner's advice for changing a left-handed to a right-handed child, as follows:

1. The changeover is advisable for karmic reasons, in order to develop a correct Earth mentality.

2. One can only change over until the ninth or tenth year; later than that it is questionable.

3. The child can continue to draw and paint with the left hand. Only the capacities that have to do with the intellect are brought over to the right hand (writing and conventional matters, such as holding a spoon).

4. One has to effect the changeover slowly (one has to allow more time for the child to do his writing in class) and simultaneously one must do artistic, pedagogical and therapeutic eurythmy exercises.

5. One then has to watch out for 'flightiness of ideas', thinking that 'stumbles'. If these symptoms occur, one must stop in the attempt to change the child's handedness.

[3] in M. Sovak *Pedagogische Probleme der Lateralitat* (*Volk und Gesundheit*, Berlin)

In practice, one will, of course, examine the whole 'sidedness' (laterality) of the child: hands, eyes, feet, ears. If everything is left-sided, then one has a 'fixed left-handedness'. A changeover will meet with little prospect of success. I will then try to examine what possible movement the right hand has (through drawing and dexterity exercises). I will ask for neurological examinations and an electroencephalogram (EEG). When we plan to change a child over, we always need a doctor who is familiar with these problems.

Dr. Rudolf Braumiller
Kraeherwald Waldorf School
Stuttgart, West Germany

Rudolf Steiner's Indications in Conferences and Lectures
Correspondences between Microcosm and Macrocosm

From the lecture of April 9, 1920 (GA 201)

We, so to speak, divide our organism into a left and a right half, because we constantly do different things with the left sense organism than with the right. You can judge this to be so if you observe that you will always do something with the left sense organ which is akin, as in thinking, to a kind of touching of an object. With the right sense organ you, as it were, 'touch' your touching. Only thus does it become your own, your possession. We could never come to a concept of the ego if we could not perceive with the right what we experience with the left. By crossing our hands over each other we get a picture of ego representation.

Renewal of the Art of Pedagogy through Spiritual Science

From the lecture of May 7, 1920 (GA 302)

Here I come to the question which has been put to me and it is one of great significance, the question of lefthandedness and ambidexterity.

It has become common human practice to be righthanded. One uses this to learn to write and to become otherwise skilled in life. It is perfectly justifiable that one also tries to make the left hand somewhat dexterous. But, when one argues about these things, it is only a fruitful discussion if one has a deeper insight into the circumstances of life. If one imagines how we are supposed to anticipate an age that could awaken human beings toward their full humanity, if we live toward an age in which we add the culture of our feelings and the activity of our will to the abstract thinking that we have developed so well today, then one is allowed to speak quite differently about these questions than one is able to nowadays. If human beings continue to be educated the way they are today, which gets them 'stuck' in abstractions (materialism is just what makes one get stuck in abstractions), if one does not grasp that the material comes from the spirit then, after a time, if we develop both hands equally for writing, we will see a certain degree of feeble-mindedness taking hold of humanity. The way we are as human beings today is very much connected to the fact that we use the right hand more extensively than the left. Our make-up depends very much on the fact that certain organs are not made symmetrically. This means that we interfere deeply in our whole human organism if we, for example, use both hands for writing.

I would not be speaking about these matters if I had not done a great deal of research into these matters; if I had not tried, for example, to see what it means to use the left hand. If one has gained any perception of human beings, one can find out for oneself what it means to use the left hand. The left hand is very good when the soul-spiritual part of the human being has reached a certain degree of independence from his physical being. In the way man today is dependent on the bodily element, we can experience an enormous revolution in the physical itself when we, for example, try to use the left hand in the same way for writing as the right hand: such a load is placed on the right side of the body and the right side of the head which the human being of today is not used to. If one uses the methods of education which applied to the human being the elements of education that we have discussed here, then a certain degree of ambidexterous use of the limbs may be allowed. Today's culture must not go over to a use of both hands out of abstract ideas. One can say these things only from experience. Statistics would essentially confirm what I have said today.

Here one also has to say: it is necessary to look into the spiritual world if one wants to gain some concept of how the spiritual-soul element in a child works together with the bodily-physical. This is especially the reason why we promise ourselves so much from eurythmy in child education, because eurythmy is an 'ensouled' movement. Through eurythmy, the activity of will is lifted up, as opposed to the mere passivity of the will which we primarily train in 'physiological' gymnastics.

Conferences with Teachers of the Free Waldorf School
June 14, 1920 (GA 300/1)

Dr. Steiner: Yes, on the whole one will find that children with spiritual predispositions can write unhampered just as they like, left and right. Children who are materialistic will become idiots if they write with both hands. There is a definite reason for righthandedness. In this materialistic age, it is a fact that children will become idiotic through lefthandedness, or when both hands are used alternately. In certain circumstances, this is a very serious matter, especially with all things that involve the intellect; this is not so with drawing. One can easily let children draw with either or both hands.

May 10, 1922 (GA 300/2)

A music teacher: May I ask a question about the beginning of piano lessons, because of the effect on both hands?

Dr. Steiner: That is a correct insight. We can easily correct lefthandedness with piano practice. One really has to pay attention to this. We should always correct lefthandedness. Then we should also pay attention to the temperament. With the melancholics, we should stress the right hand. With them, one will easily find a tendency to play with the left hand. With a choleric, we should also stress the right hand. With a phlegmatic, we would have to balance both hands equally and the same is true with sanguine children. That would be important.

One would also have to try to see that children will not merely get a mechanical feeling for piano playing, but that they will learn to feel the piano keys as such. They should feel the different areas on the piano, whether up or down, right or left. To begin with, it is very good to let them play without written music.

May 25, 1923 (GA 300/3)

He is asked if one should wean children of lefthandedness.

Dr. Steiner: As a rule, yes! Before the ninth year, one can get children used to righthandedness in all school subjects. It would not be right to do this if it became harmful, which could be the case in some instances. Children are not a sum total, but a complicated potency. If one would want to bring about symmetry between right and left, if one would practice with both hands equally, it could lead to feeble-mindedness in later years.

The phenomenon of lefthandedness is distinctly a phenomenon of karma, a phenomenon of karmic weakness. I will take an example: a person has been under tremendous strain in his previous life, not just through physical or intellectual work, but also through spiritual or soul stress. This person is then born into this life with a strong weakness — the part of the human being that has to do with life between death and a new birth concentrates itself especially in the lower part of man; the part of man which has more to do with the head organization comes more from a previous life. He now has to try to overcome the karmic weakness in his lower part. Therefore, that which is usually developed strongly becomes weak and, as a substitute for this weakness, the left leg and the left hand are especially engaged in order to help. The predominance of the left hand now leads to the fact that, instead of the left, the right cerebral convolution is developed for speech.

If one gives in to this weakness, then it can be that this weakness will stay, also for a later, perhaps even the third, incarnation after this one. If one does not give in, one can again create a balance.

If one asks a child to do everything equally: writing, drawing, working, then we 'neutralize' the inner man to such an extent that the ego and astral body are lifted out and the person becomes completely 'limp' in later life. In any case, the ether body is much stronger on the left side; the astral body is developed more strongly on the right side. One cannot get around this and must take it into consideration. One must not attempt a 'mechanical equalization'. It is dilettantism when one strives to work with both hands equally. The fact that people today try to develop both hands equally is related to the complete ignorance of the nature of the human being.

December 18, 1923 (GA 300/3)

X: One of my students in the 7th grade makes more and faster progress in writing with the left hand than with the right.

Dr. Steiner: One should draw her attention to the fact that she should only be allowed to write with the right hand. You can try to let her sit on her haunches on her right, no, her left, leg, so that she jumps with the right leg. She should jump with the right leg while her left leg is pulled up. She is ambidextrous.

When we have clearly pronounced left-handed people, then we have to make a decision. One can observe this. One must observe the left hand. With truly left-handed people, the hands look as if they have been exchanged. The left hand looks like the right hand. The left has more lines in it than the right one.

One can combat this with the eyes. Children who are truly lefthanded have to be asked to look at their right arm from the top, then one allows the eyes to travel all the way down until they have arrived at the right hand, and then one allows the eyes to travel upward again. Then one asks them to stretch out the right arm. This is repeated three times.

Meditative Observations and Indications to Deepen the Art of Therapy

Lecture of January 8, 1924 (GA 316)

Chiromancy looks at these matters similarly, just as it does with the hair and the iris of the eye. But one has to have inspiration for this and not the superficial rules that are commonly given. We need a quite specific predisposition, which some people have, in order to explore the lines of the hand. They are intimately connected with human development. You need only compare how the lines of your own right or left hand look. In ordinary life, it is obvious that a person writes with the right and not with the left hand. Is that not so? There is a difference. If one is inspired to do so, one can see the whole karma of the human being in the left hand. In the right hand, we see the personal industry and what the human being has accomplished in this lifetime. His fate has created his life on earth, and his accomplishments lead him into the future. These things are not without deeper reasons, but it is dangerous to represent them to the public because we tread here on ground where seriousness and dilettantism border closely on each other. Some other things will still result as a natural consequence of our observations.

Anthroposophical Pedagogy and its Prerequisites

Questions and Answers, April 15, 1924 (GA 309)

Question: How does one introduce writing to left-handed children?

Dr. Steiner: It is necessary for us to do a great deal to change a left-handed to a right-handed person. Even when one sees that, out of one's practice, one has not succeeded, one should continue to go on working with lefthandedness. It should be the only, much-desired goal to change 'lefties' to righthandedness; essentially, we will succeed with this, especially in writing, in the 'drawing' of letters. In general, it is, of course, necessary that we strongly observe such a child when we are trying to change from left to righthandedness. One has to observe how, at a certain stage, the child shows a tendency toward flighty ideas. He can also begin to think too fast and, therefore, bring himself to 'stumbling' with his thoughts. One has to observe this carefully and draw the children's attention to it, because the connection between arm, hand, and speech-center development is much more important for the development of the whole human being than is commonly thought; many other things have an influence on whether a child is right or lefthanded.

Question: Is it advisable to let children between the tenth and twelfth year practice mirror writing?

Dr. Steiner: Why it should be advisable to allow children between ten and twelve to practice mirror writing is beyond my comprehension. I cannot imagine that it is desirable in any life circumstances! If one rises toward spiritual vision, one will get, in any case, something like a mirror picture of that which acts like an after-effect of physical life. It is indeed a fact that, if one carries something in a written way into the spiritual world, it will appear there (above) into the future. These things are not without deeper reasons, but it is dangerous to represent them to the public because we tread here on ground where seriousness and dilettantism border closely on each other. Some other things will still result as a natural consequence of our observations.

Anthroposophical Pedagogy and its Prerequisites

Questions and Answers, April 15, 1924
(GA 309)

Question: How does one introduce writing to left-handed children?

Dr. Steiner: It is necessary for us to do a great deal to change a left-handed to a right-handed person. Even when one sees that, out of one's practice, one has not succeeded, one should continue to go on working with lefthandedness. It should be the only, much-desired goal to change 'lefties' to righthandedness; essentially, we will succeed with this, especially in writing, the 'drawing' of letters. In general, it is, we strongly change from left to righthandedness. One has to observe how, at a certain stage, the child shows a tendency toward flighty ideas. He can also begin to think too fast and, therefore, bring himself to 'stumbling' with his thoughts. One has to observe this carefully and draw the children's attention to it, because the connection between arm, hand, and speech-center development is much more important for the development of the whole human being than is commonly thought; many other things have an influence on whether a child is right or lefthanded.

Question: Is it advisable to let children between the tenth and twelfth year practice mirror writing?

Dr. Steiner: Why it should be advisable to allow children between ten and twelve to practice mirror writing is beyond my comprehension. I cannot imagine that it is desirable in any life circumstances! If one rises toward spiritual vision, one will get, in any case, something like a mirror picture of that which acts like an after-effect of physical life. It is indeed a fact tha *j*
carries somethin

as mirror picture. Let us take an example: let us say — I will be quite free in speaking about these things — someone would try to turn to someone who has gone through death, and let us try to imagine that one would need something in writing in order to compare what one has experienced with this personality. In such a case, the writing as one knows it here, as it is written here, will appear as if one would be reading mirror writing. Writing as it is normally written in the physical will appear as its mirror picture when one looks into the spiritual world. If one were to teach a child artificially to write mirror writing, one would make it a stranger to the earth, one would especially estrange the child from the use of his head. One should not do this. This could, under certain circumstances, lead to considerable spiritual and psychic disturbances. Anthroposophical pedagogy is especially aimed at preparing people for physical life, not to lead them into cloud-cuckoo-lands. To teach a child to write mirror writing would tear the child out of physical life.

Question: Why is it that the direction in which European languages are written is from left to right; in Hebrew from right to left and, in Chinese, from above down?

Dr. Steiner: We are led into great depths of cultural history when we look at the arrangement of writing from left to right, and so forth. At the most, one can only give a small indication.

In previous ages of human evolution, there was an instinctive vision present in human beings. People, indeed, did not see physical occurrences as intensively as we see them now. Instead they saw more of what lived as spirit in the physical. We usually do not imagine how differently from today the human being looked into the world in olden times. People think so easily that, when an ancient Greek looked up into the sky and saw blue (which is so much more intense in the south than in the north), that he saw the same beauty as the present-day Greek sees. That is not the case. The ancient Greek eye did not have such a living impression of blue. We can prove this by the fact that the word 'blue' is missing for the ancient Greeks. They saw everything more in red and yellow nuances; they saw the sky as more greenish than bluish. The whole life of soul, insofar as it is dependent on the senses, has changed in the course of time.

Hebrew has rightly been called one of the languages which has a living connection with archetypal human writing. Therefore, they have preserved the direction from right to left, which we have only kept in doing sums; we also have this as an inheritance of our civilization, a much older inheritance than our handwriting. But we do not notice this any more. We add and subtract, which is also derived from the Orient; we write numbers from left to right, but the nature of the numbers themselves demands that we sum them up from right to left. From this you can see that our numbering system is of much older origin than our writing system. This is what one can say about this.

If you then take Chinese writing: well, you will then have to keep in mind all the habits of Chinese culture. We have certain things quite alive in us, such as the circling of the earth in the direction from left to right, or from right to left. The Chinese do not have these things in their feelings in the same way. In the direction from below up or from above down, the Chinese have the very oldest direction into which human feeling can penetrate.

Lectures to Workmen at the Goetheanum

Lecture of August 2, 1922 (GA 347)

We meet blood vessels and nerve fibers in the left brain convolution, the so-called speech center, just as in any other part of the human body. Perceptions and impressions work on the nerve fibers. The movements which the child makes when pronouncing sounds are transmitted through the nerves to the left speech-convolution. The speech center is hereby well developed by having the breath work together with the blood. It works together with what emanates from the ear, but also from the eye. This process eventually orders the brain matter in a beautiful way.

From this, you can see that the brain is actually only formed, at least in these areas (but it is really the same for all areas of the brain), by the fact that perception works together with another activity, namely, the thrust which drives the blood into the brain.

Now, you will also have to clear up the following: the child learns to speak in this fashion, that it forms its left brain-convolution. If one sits by a corpse and dissects it, one can see that the right brain-convolution, which is symmetrical to the left, is relatively undeveloped. We have, therefore, a brain-convolution which is very beautiful, as I have told you; but the right brain-convolution remains throughout life as it was in the child. It remains undifferentiated. I would like to say that if we only had the right brain-convolution, we could only scream: we can speak, because we prepare our left brain-convolution so especially.

Now you see that if a person is left-handed, if he is not in the habit of performing his work with his right hand but with his left, then the curious fact emerges that, when he has a stroke on the left side, he does not lose his speech. If he were then dissected, one would find that, in him, the left-handed person, the right brain-convolution is ordered in a way such as it is ordinarily in normal right-handed people with their left brain-convolution.

Therefore, hand and arm movements

play an extraordinary part in the development of the brain. How does this happen? This happens because, if a person gets used to doing a lot with the right hand, he does not only do things with his right hand, but he gets used to breathing a little more strongly to use more breath-energy. He gets used to hearing more clearly on the right side, and so forth. This shows us that the human being has a tendency to exert more effort on his right side if he has the tendency to use the right, rather than the left hand. We have developed the left brain-convolution when we are righthanded and the right brain-convolution if we are lefthanded. Whence does this come?

Well, you see (he is drawing), when we have on the body the right hand, the right arm, then we have here in the head the left brain-convolution. Then we must examine how the nerves run. The nerves run thus: here, inside, you have nerves everywhere. For instance, if you did not have the nerves here inside, you would not feel warmth or cold. This is all connected with the nerves. Here, we have nerves everywhere. The nerves emerge from the spinal column and go into the brain. But the curious fact is that the nerves of the right hand go into the left brain, and the nerves of the left hand go into the right brain. Inside, there is namely a crossing of the nerves. The nerves cross themselves in the brain. Therefore, if I, for instance, do a certain gymnastic exercise or a eurythmy exercise with the right hand or right arm, then I feel this through the fact that the nerve transmits this feeling, that I feel it with the left half of the brain, because the nerves cross themselves.

Now, let us imagine that a child prefers to do everything with the right hand, then he breathes a little more strongly with the right side, hears a little more sharply on the right side. The human being exerts himself a little more on the right side and, therefore, the motivation for his movements is developed in his left brain.

You can also imagine how we all have some habits, such as following our speech with gestures. "Ah!" (as in "star") (accompanying gesture): and when we want to push something away: "E" (pronounced like the English letter "A") (as in "take") (translator). We make the gesture while we speak. These gestures are felt by our nerves. The gestures of the right hand, which we make while we speak, are felt by the left side of the brain.

We also have the tendency, if we are righthanded, to enunciate the vowels and consonants more strongly with the right side of the larynx. We speak the sounds more strongly; then we feel what we are doing more strongly with the left side of the brain. This is the reason why the brain is more differentiated. Originally, the brain was merely a 'mush'. We leave the left side more unused; therefore, the right brain half is less developed, stays 'mushier'; but if we have a left-handed person, the whole is reversed.

This brings about a number of important pedagogical consequences. You must image that, when one has left-handed children in school (we have these in fewer numbers but we have them), then the right temporal lobe is in full development whereas, with all others, the left temporal lobe is developed quite artistically. If I teach these children to write, then I have them use the right hand for writing. Those children who are righthanded will be reinforced in the development of that which they have already developed when they learned to speak, namely, the left lobe. But if I force those children who are left-handed to write with the right hand, it will ruin that which they have embedded in the right temporal lobe through speech. They spoil this again and, therefore, I have the task of leading what they do with the left hand slowly and gradually into the right hand. It is not so that one should let the lefthanded write with the left. They first have to learn to *work* with the other hand, and then they will get into writing, even if it is much slower for them than it is for other children. It does not matter if they learn to write a little later.

If I allow left-handed children to learn to write with their right hand as fast as right-handed ones, then I will make them more stupid, because I spoil what they have developed in the right half of the brain.

I must, therefore, take care that children who are lefthanded are taught to write with their right hand in a way different from those who are righthanded. They will then not become more stupid in later life, but more intelligent. I must lead the lefthandedness *slowly* into righthandedness and not just confuse the brain by simply having them write with the right hand.

If one wants to treat the whole human

being only through writing, then pedagogically one will reach the opposite from what one wants to achieve. Nowadays, there is a great tendency to teach people everything with both hands, to let them do everything with both hands. Then I confuse everything in the brain. It merely shows how few people know about this tendency, if they let the person do the same things with the right and the left.

From a Lecture to the Workmen
February 9, 1924 (GA 352)

You see, we human beings are really always two persons. We are several human beings: I have told you — physical man, etheric man, and so forth. But simply in our physical being, we are already two persons: a right one and a left one. The right side of the body is enormously different from the left. I believe that very few of you who are sitting here could write with the left hand; we write with the right hand. But that part, for instance, which is connected with speech through the nervous system is located in the left half of the brain. There are well-defined convolutions there, but not on the right side. With the left-handed person, this is reversed. Those who are lefthanded have their speech organization on the right side; not the outer organization, only the inner one, which stimulates speech. One can, therefore, say: the human being is very different on the right side from what he is on the left side. But this is also true in other ways. The heart is more toward the left, the stomach and liver toward the right. But also those organs which are otherwise symmetrical are really not quite symmetrical. Our lungs have two lobes on the left and three lobes on the right. Therefore, the right man is very different from the left one. How does this happen? Let us start with something very simple. We usually do not learn to write with the left hand, but with the right. This is an activity which depends more on the ether body. The physical body is heavier, it is more developed on the left. The ether body is more developed on the right. The left forms two lobes; the right, which is more active, brings more life into the lung and develops three lobes in the lung. The human being is, on the left, a more physical being and, on the right, a more etheric one. It is also thus with speech: nutrition in the brain is more necessary with right-handed people on the left side than on the right. Much is arranged with the human being so that he has more earth forces on the left and, on the right, he has the more etheric forces of heaven.

Our present science, which tries to see only matter and, therefore, does not know much about the material, educates children's left and right in the same way. Well, human beings are simply not made for this! If one exaggerates this trend, then one can say that people today are being educated to become crazy. The human body is so arranged that it is more physical on the left and more etheric on the right. But what does our present science care about whether something is physical or etheric! Both the right and the left human being are the same for them. These things have to be penetrated with spiritual science if one wants in any way to begin to understand them. Therefore: on the left, the human being is more earthly, on the right, he is more heavenly, cosmic (if one wants to call it that without being misunderstood).

Man has already strongly emancipated himself. He has developed the left — earthly, and the right—heavenly, halves in such a way that he can carry them around as a physical person; also in such a way that one does not notice any more that the left inclines toward the earth and the right toward heaven. There are people who have a tendency more toward the earth; they sleep mostly on the left side, lie down on the left side. Most people lie down on the right side, either when they are tired of the left or when they are busy with the powers that tend more toward heaven. Such things are, of course, difficult to observe because there are still other considerations involved. If the right side of the room is darker, then a person might also prefer to lie on the right. That, too, is a reason. It is difficult to merely observe through thoughts and other such things, but altogether it is quite true that a person has a tendency to lie down, to sleep, on the left side, because it is the earthly side.

Further lectures by Rudolf Steiner in which he deals with the qualities 'left-right':

| Gesamt-Ausgabe | Titel | Vortrage vom |

Bibl-Nr.
115 Anthroposophie-Psychosophie-
　　Pneumatosophie　　　　　　　26.10.1909
158 Der Zusammenhang des Menschen
　　mit der elementarischen welt　21.11.1914
184 Die Polaritat von Dauer und
　　Entwicklung im Menschenleben　20.9.1918
201 Entsprechungen zwischen
　　Mikrokosmos und
　　Makrokosmos　　　　9., 10., 11.4.1920
348 Uber Gesundheit und Krankheit　16.12.1922
326 Der Entstehungsmoment der
　　Naturwissenschaft　　　　　　26.12.1922
277 Eurythmie–Die Offenbarung　　30.12.1923 ⎱
　　der sprechenden Seele　　　　2. 2.1924 ⎰
278 Eurythmie als sichtbarer
　　Gesang　　　　　　　19., 21., 26. 2.1924

FROM THE THERAPEUTIC EURYTHMY WORK WITH LEFT-HANDED CHILDREN

First of all, I should like to describe the children with whom I worked from 1922 until 1969 at the Waldorf schools in Hamburg-Wandsbek and Benefeld.

Left-handed children are a very endearing folk. They are delicate. This is evident from the fact that they are often absent from school. They do not have any marked symptoms of illness, but they have little resistance. They have so-called 'indispositions.' They are easily cold, and most of them cannot concentrate. It has happened that they have approached me in the middle of an exercise to admire a piece of jewelry or the color of a dress I was wearing. Or they discovered something beautiful and new in the therapeutic eurythmy room. I knew that, if I brought a new flower pot or a new picture or something similar into the room, the left-handed children would be the first to discover it. It had to be something beautiful above all else, and they had to communicate this to me immediately. Manually, they were rather awkward. They took longer to master the exercises. One could confirm the popular expression, someone is a 'lefty.' There were also many little 'dummlings' among them who created a good deal of work for their class teachers. They clung to me and also had the urge to tell me all the happenings of the previous day, and I had to exercise great diplomacy in that I arranged it so that today one, and tomorrow another, was allowed to tell me their tales, but only after the exercises. But, even so, they sometimes burst out with it in the middle of a lesson.

Among others, I once had a pair of twins in school who were both lefthanded. There was also a boy who painted beautifully. His grandfather was also a painter and also lefthanded. One often finds lefthandedness among artists.

One always noticed that they were looking for physical and soul warmth. When they arrived and when they left, they always wanted cuddling. They expected to be lovingly noticed.

Further, in contrast to the dyslexic, the left-handed children were all somewhat similar. One has to treat dyslexics with more reserve and with a little more 'distance.'

I would like to pass on some indications which I received from Dr. Karl Koenig:

One should, first of all, determine whether one is dealing with a purely left-handed child — if the left eye, ear and left foot dominate. How does one determine this? Let them hammer a nail, sharpen a pencil, cut bread, throw something with one hand, push something away with a foot, climb on a chair, look through a tube, or a hole in a piece of paper (the child chooses the eye which aims!). Let them listen to the soft ticking of a watch (without your leading the watch to their ears!).

If one has a mixed dominance, then it is especially important to change the 'sidedness' to the right. With a mixed dominance, the ego, so to speak, makes constant zig-zags from one side to the other. One must change this at the right time.

Dominance of the hands is only developed after the third and fourth year of life. One can already stimulate a change during childhood play. One has to do this very gently, so that the child will not start to stutter or become nervous. One should only attempt to make the change up to the ninth year.

Dr. Koenig related to us that statistics show that 49% of all people are righthanded, 5.3% are purely lefthanded, and 46.7% have mixed dominance.

With completely left-handed children, a doctor should be consulted before attempting to make the change to righthandedness.

Now to the exercises:

To begin, I A O, 2/4 beat walking, then vowels, only with the right side (this was the advice Rudolf Steiner gave to Frau Daehnhardt, therapeutic eurythmist at the Waldorf School in Stuttgart). In standing and walking, take care that the left arm rests well while the right exercises; perhaps the left hand can hold the dress or pants.

Throw a rod with the right hand and take a firm step with the right foot simultaneously toward the eurythmist: let down the right arm, pull the left foot forward (to meet the right foot—*translator*).

Exercises of Dr. Karl Schubert, from the special class of the Waldorf School: "With the right I want to write"; one steps forward with a firm step, walking the stressed syllables with a kind of I-movement (sounds like the English letter E in the word 'see'—*translator*) with the right arm: the left foot is drawn forward after the short interval toward the beginning position. "With the left I let it rest"; the same left, arm down and going backward with it.

"With the right I fight"; walk with energy, emphasize right, move right arm in I-movement forward, the right hand making a fist. "With the left I carry"; softly going forward, left step, left hand first, arm making a loving, inward gesture.

Two exercises by Rudolf Steiner from the conference of December 18, 1923: the first exercises must have been for a 12- to 13-year-old girl.

A further indication by Rudolf Steiner: throw the right arm three times upward and outward, three times right leg forward and outward, at the same time hop on the left leg in order to throw out the astral body, which is blocking the limbs.

Rudolf Steiner told the class teacher to allow left-handed children to hop toward a 'goal' with outstretched right arm and right leg.

These are strenuous and one-sided exercises, oriented toward the right. I had the experience that I would like to gradually lead these exercises back to 'eurythmetizing' with both arms, to place them, so to speak, back into three dimensions.

I also did the following exercises:

Seven-part rod exercise, twelve-part rod exercise, walking rhythms and beat, evolution series, first half of sound right, then half a sound left, then whole sound with both arms.

The big E exercise, dexterity E (as in *say*); L in walking, mirror-picture forms, harmonic eight for two, L-M for outbreathing, A-reverence which helps to stimulate forces of resistance. The position of 'Libra' and C. I took reference to the preceding text of April 9, 1920; otherwise, I did not use the zodiac or planetary gestures with children; but this Libra and C movement gives peace and lightness simultaneously.

Ilse Rolofs

EXPERIENCES WITH A LEFT-HANDED CHILD

A.T., born May 1, 1968

A small boy was taken into the first grade in the Fall of 1974. Aside from other insecurities, he was definitely left-oriented. He came from a cultured home, he was an only a child, a little spoiled, and gave the impression of being, on the whole, very young for a first grader. (His sixth birthday was exactly two months before the cut-off date.)

He was among the smaller children in height. He made a dreamy impression during lessons; his gestures still had a lot of the soft roundedness of the small child in them. According to the mother, he had been slow of speech in his third year.

Four months after the beginning of the second school year, I received A. into the small group of somewhat backward children for therapeutic eurythmy. They had to be awakened. I also received strict instructions that A. was to remain left-handed! An inquiry with the school doctor had resulted in the fact that he really used his left arm and leg as well as eye and ear spontaneously. So we stamped and clapped, threw the ball in rhythm, and so on. A. did everything diligently on the left, whatever the other children did on the right. He did the dexterity-E well with both feet.

After a time, A.'s parents asked that he be given violin lessons. Now the struggle started for his right hand with the bow. This was the occasion for the whole problem to be brought up once again with the mother and doctor. Before making a final decision, one was going to take an electro-encephalogram (EEG). But long before the result of this test was known, something strange happened in the therapeutic eurythmy lesson: A. was looking at the ball in my hands, looked at his own, turned around in order to stand in the same direction as I was, turned back, moved his hands alternately, caught the ball — and threw it with the right hand! He repeated this several times. It also happened that he moved his right foot clearly on the emphasis of the word.

Nothing was now clearer than, with all the consequences that might follow, to try to change him to the right before his ninth year! He had the most difficulty in writing with the right hand. He needed much encouragement, because it was never beautiful enough for him.

The result of the EEG proved that he had a disturbance in the brain. But, strangely enough, it was on the right side. Throughout the second and into the third school year, A. did concentration exercises and therapeutic eurythmy, as well as changing rhythms: LM, big E (as in s*ay*) exercise, variations on A (as in st*ar*) and also the so-called lefthandedness exercises: "With the right, I want to write ..."; jumping on the left leg and simultaneously throwing out the right arm and leg; letting a horizontal rod drop out of the right hand, catching it again before it touched the floor; with the gaze (Rudolf Steiner: eye-crossing) going slowly down the right arm from shoulder to fingers and following it back again. According to the class teacher, A. became very much 'at home' on the right side.

Brigitte Schuerholz